COBBLESTONE · THE CIVIL WAR

Jefferson Davis

And the Confederacy

Cobblestone Publishing
A Division of Carus Publishing
Peterborough, NH
www.cobblestonepub.com

Staff

Editorial Director: Lou Waryncia

Editor: Sarah Elder Hale

Book Design: David Nelson, www.dnelsondesign.com

Proofreaders: Meg Chorlian, Eileen Terrill

Text Credits

The content of this volume is derived from articles that first appeared in *COBBLESTONE* magazine. Contributors: Robin Belesky, Craig E. Blohm, Gabor S. Boritt, Kelly Clark, Stephen Currie, Betty J. Gair, Gwendolyn Green, Sarah Elder Hale, Robert L. Hawkins, III, Harold Holzer, Kathiann M. Kowalski, Mark E. M. Neely Jr., Evelyn W. West.

Picture Credits

Photos.com: 3; Beauvoir, the Jefferson Davis Home and Presidential Library, Biloxi, Mississippi: 4, 14, 41, 43; Library of Congress: 5, 6, 8, 9, 10, 11, 17, 18, 19, 20, 22, 23, 27, 28, 29, 30, 31, 32, 37, 39, 40, 42; Clipart.com: 7, 12, 13, 15, 16, 21, 34, 38 (bottom), 40 (inset); Fred Carlson: 24–25, 44–45; Robin Hansen: 35. Images for "Civil War Time Line," pages 44–45, courtesy of Photos.com, Clipart.com, and Library of Congress.

Cover

Louis Mathieu Didier Guillaume, *Jefferson Davis Reviewing a Louisiana Regiment at Richmond, VA*

Courtesy of R.W. Norton Art Gallery, Shreveport, Louisiana

Library of Congress Cataloging-in-Publication Data for
Jefferson Davis and the Confederacy is available at http://catalog.loc.gov.

Printed in China

Cobblestone Publishing

30 Grove Street, Suite C

Peterborough, NH 03458

www.cobblestonepub.com

Table of Contents

Young Jefferson Davis 4

A Promising Officer 7

The Colonel From Mississippi.................................10

Family Ties 12

The Statesman Emerges 15

A Nation Divided...19

Secession!...23

Map: The War Between the States 24

The Confederate President: Was Davis Doomed to Defeat?......26

Raiders, Cruisers, and Blockade Runners 31

A Spy in the Confederate White House.................................35

The Confederate Image: Art of the Civil War South..................37

Symbol of the Lost Cause 40

Civil War Time Line 44

Glossary 46

Index................................47

Young Jefferson Davis

Jefferson Davis was born on June 3, 1808, the youngest of 10 children. His father, Samuel Emory Davis, named him after Thomas Jefferson, the third U.S. president.

At the time of Jefferson's birth, the Davis family lived near Fairview, Kentucky. When the family farm there proved too small and unproductive, Samuel decided to move farther west. They went to the Louisiana Territory in 1810. The following year, when Jefferson was almost three years old, the family settled in Woodville, which was in the Mississippi Territory. The Davises named their home Rosemont.

Davis's contemporaries thought he was handsome. He grew to be 5 feet 11 inches tall and was known for always standing perfectly straight.

A Good Education

Samuel strongly believed in providing his children with a good education. But, at that time, there were no free public schools. So, Jefferson attended a one-room schoolhouse with his sister Mary Ellen, where they were taught by their older brother Benjamin.

Then, in 1816, at age eight, Jefferson traveled to Springfield, Kentucky, to attend St. Thomas College, a Catholic school operated by Dominican friars. There were not many educational opportunities in Mississippi. Samuel knew that the Catholics maintained the finest schools in the South, and he wanted his youngest son to have the best education.

On the way to Kentucky, Jefferson and his traveling companions, Colonel Thomas Hinds and his son, Howell, stopped in Nashville, Tennessee, for a two-week visit at the home of Andrew Jackson. Young Jefferson was quite impressed with Jackson, a popular general from the War of 1812, who was a gracious host and kind to the boys.

After two years at St. Thomas, Jefferson's mother missed him and wanted him to come home. Boarding his first steamship down the Mississippi River, Jefferson set out for Natchez, Mississippi, which was the closest riverboat stop to Rosemont. He eventually enrolled in nearby Wilkinson County Academy.

When not attending boarding schools, Davis lived at his family home, Rosemont. He and his brothers and sisters enjoyed playing in the woods, orchards, and fields of their Mississippi plantation.

Andrew Jackson
(1767–1845)

Always popular in his state for the justice he championed as a lawyer and judge, Jackson became a national hero when he led the Tennessee militia to victory over the British at the end of the War of 1812. His popularity won him the presidency and made his life seem a true expression of the American dream. He had risen, through his own determination, from being a penniless lawyer to the highest office in the land.

The election of Jackson was a triumph of ordinary people over the aristocratic, educated elite. America's first six presidents had come from long-established families in prosperous eastern communities. Andrew Jackson, the seventh president of the United States (1829–1837), had been born on the Carolina frontier, had had little education, and had made his way in the barely civilized state of Tennessee.

Jacksonian democracy, as his politics came to be called, was based on his belief in the right of the people to self-government. "The people are sovereign," he said. "Their will is absolute." His ideas brought a democracy of the common man to the country.

A Lesson in Hard Work

But Jefferson grew bored with his studies at the academy. One day after an argument with the headmaster of the academy, Jefferson decided to quit school. When Jefferson told his father about the disagreement and his decision to stop attending school, Samuel remained cool-headed. He told Jefferson that no one at Rosemont would be idle. Jefferson was put to work in the fields picking cotton. After only a few days of this chore, he decided that school was not so bad after all. The incident gave Jefferson a new appreciation for learning.

By 1821, a series of crop failures depleted Samuel's finances. He could no longer afford to send Jefferson to school. At the suggestion of his father, Jefferson asked his brother Joseph for financial help. Joseph, 23 years older than Jefferson, did not have any sons of his own. He agreed to pay for his youngest brother's schooling. In 1823, Jefferson entered Transylvania University in Lexington, Kentucky.

During this time, Joseph was the primary influence in Jefferson's life. When Jefferson had time off from school, he stayed with Joseph at his plantation, The Hurricane. Jefferson Davis learned the importance of family and education at an early age. These values would remain with him throughout his life.

A Promising Officer

In 1824, at the age of 16, Jefferson Davis had two educational goals. First, he planned to finish his senior year at Transylvania University, the boarding school he was attending. Then, he would study law at the University of Virginia. Once he finished his education, he probably would become a lawyer and a planter like his brother Joseph.

On to West Point

Davis's family, however, wanted him to have a military career. His brother used his influence with

Mississippi politicians to get Jefferson accepted to the U.S. Military Academy at West Point, New York. Being admitted to West Point was an honor. It also was difficult: There were perhaps 30 applicants for every available spot. Still, Davis was far from thrilled. He reluctantly left his school in Kentucky and accepted the military school position only when his family agreed to let him leave after one year if he chose.

As it turned out, Davis enjoyed his time at West Point. In fact, he may have enjoyed it too much. As one biographer put it, Davis's behavior "was not the most exemplary." He often got into trouble for drinking, sneaking out at night, and violating other West Point codes of behavior. Davis was not a very strong student, either. Though he excelled in a few subjects, such as French and drawing, he performed poorly in mathematics. Moreover, the time he spent

Davis reluctantly arrived at the U.S. Military Academy at West Point at age 16. He stayed there for four years, and was better known for his popularity and mischief-making than for his academic record.

7

breaking the rules and reading novels interfered with his ability to do homework. The result: Davis graduated in the bottom half of his class and began his Army life in 1828 as a low-ranking second lieutenant.

A Respect for Native Americans

Over the next few years, Davis served at various Army outposts near the upper Mississippi River. These were not easy times for Davis. The winters were brutally cold, and the distance from family and friends was great. In addition, his duties involved very little soldiering. Instead, Davis spent his time overseeing sawmills and supervising the building of forts. The only fighting he encountered was against the region's Native Americans. Davis had misgivings about the Army's battles with the Native Americans. He thought that white settlers and the U.S. Army treated them unfairly, and he disapproved of the harsh policies in effect against them. In Davis's view, there was much to admire about the native people — their military strategies, their courage, and their ability to live off the land. Writing years later of a conflict with the Sauk and Fox tribes under the leadership of the great Indian chief Black Hawk, Davis concluded, "The real heroes were Black Hawk and his savages."

Black Hawk, chief of the Sauk tribe, was caught between white settlers from the East and rival native tribes in the West. Jefferson Davis, a young army officer at the time, admired Black Hawk, and he disagreed with the government's efforts to disrupt the native way of life.

Coolness and Gallantry

Despite the hardships and his concerns about injustice, Davis became a respected commander. With especially strong diplomatic skills, Davis was liked and admired by his men. He also was noted for his bravery and calmness in the face of disaster. As a fellow officer summed it up, Davis was "one of the brightest and most promising officers in the whole Army." Before long, he was promoted to first lieutenant.

Nevertheless, in 1835, Davis abruptly resigned from the Army. His future in the military, Davis had concluded, was dim. The country was at peace, so there were few positions available for officers. The pay was poor, too. Besides, Davis wanted to marry and start a family. His intended bride had been forbidden by her father, Colonel (later General) Zachary Taylor, to marry a soldier. All these factors led to Davis's return to private life. Eleven years later, though, Davis went back to the Army. War with Mexico had broken out. Davis, then a member of the U.S. House of Representatives, volunteered to lead a Mississippi regiment into battle. "My education and former practice," he wrote, "would...enable me to be of service." The men in Davis's charge were unused to military life, but soon grew to appreciate his skills as a leader. "If he should tell his men to jump into a cannon's mouth they would think it right," wrote Davis's brother-in-law Joseph Davis Howell, who served in the regiment.

Davis and his men went on to distinguish themselves at the battles of Monterrey and Buena Vista. Davis was cheered for his courage and his command of military strategy. Taylor, the general in charge, spoke of Davis's "coolness and gallantry" under fire. Though wounded, Davis returned home a hero. Once again, his military days were over — this time, for good.

Colonel Zachary Taylor's nickname, "Old Rough and Ready," described his style of leadership: straightforward decisions and swift action. Davis married Taylor's daughter in 1835 and served under Taylor during the U.S.–Mexican War.

Jefferson Davis proved his skill as a military leader and strategist in a surprise attack on the fort La Teneria at Monterrey, Mexico.

The Colonel From Mississippi

The highlights of Jefferson Davis's military career came during the U.S.–Mexican War, where twice he showed uncommon courage and intelligence on the battlefield.

Leading the Way at Monterrey

The first indication of Davis's military talent came at the Battle of Monterrey in September 1846. Desperate to take over the Mexican fort La Teneria, General Zachary Taylor looked to Davis. The Americans already had lost three companies of soldiers to Mexican cannon. Taylor hoped Davis could find a way to turn the tide for the Americans.

Together with General John Quitman, Davis led his troops toward the fort. As smoke from guns and cannon covered the ground, Davis had his men execute a maneuver that brought them within 100 yards of La Teneria. Then, unexpectedly, Davis led a charge. Before the Mexicans could react, the Americans were inside the fort. Panicked, the Mexicans retreated, leaving La Teneria — and Monterrey — to the Americans.

Perfect Timing at Buena Vista

A few months later, Davis became a hero at the Battle of Buena Vista by charging a wing of the Mexican army led by General Pedro de Ampudia. Ampudia had just demolished another American regiment and still had a huge edge in manpower. Though Davis's timing seemed suicidal, it turned out to be perfect. Ampudia was still celebrating his earlier success and was unprepared for the Americans' maneuver. Davis's troops broke through the Mexican line and forced Ampudia's men to retreat.

Davis's bold offensive in the Battle of Buena Vista forced Mexican general Pedro de Ampudia to retreat and made Davis a hero.

Davis was not finished. Next, he set up his men in two lines that looked like the two walls of the letter "V." This formation meant the Mexicans would have to fire on Davis's men to get past them. The Mexicans had more soldiers, but Davis knew his troops had better weapons. The battle was over almost as soon as it began. When the shooting started, reported Davis, "The mass [of the Mexican Army] yielded to the blow and the survivors fled." The Americans had anticipated defeat at Buena Vista. Thanks in part to Davis, it turned out otherwise.

Family Ties

On June 17, 1835, 27-year-old Jefferson Davis married Sarah Knox Taylor. "Knox" was the daughter of Colonel Zachary Taylor, Davis's commanding officer. Because Taylor did not want his daughter to marry a military man, Davis resigned from the Army. He made plans to begin life as a planter.

Davis brought his bride home to Mississippi, but their marriage ended in tragedy. The couple became ill with malaria, and Sarah died after only three months of marriage. A grief-stricken Davis spent the next eight years in seclusion. He worked at his plantation, Brierfield, and passed long hours in the library at his brother Joseph's nearby home. The carefree youth had become a somber man.

Varina and Jefferson

Worried about his brother, Joseph arranged for Davis to meet Varina Banks

12

Howell, the daughter of a Natchez, Mississippi, planter. Although she was only 17, the intelligent, well-educated young lady won Davis's heart. On February 26, 1845, they began a marriage that would last almost 45 years.

Varina was a constant help and companion to Davis. She supported him in his political career by acting as his secretary. She even signed Davis's name on documents if he was too ill to write. As first lady of the Confederacy, Varina entertained visitors at the Confederate White House in Richmond, Virginia. She visited the sick and wounded during the Civil War.

Varina was Davis's most passionate defender. After the war, she asked the government to release Davis from Fort Monroe and even paid a personal visit to President Andrew Johnson. In the years after Davis's death, Varina fought to keep his memory alive by signing her name "Varina Jefferson Davis." She also wrote a memoir of her husband, *Jefferson Davis, Ex-President of the Confederate States of America: A Memoir by His Wife*.

For most of the Civil War, the capital of the Confederate States of America was Richmond, Virginia. The Davis family lived at the Confederate White House on the corner of 12th and Clay streets.

The Davis Children

Davis and Varina had six children: Samuel, Margaret, Jefferson, Jr., Joseph, William, and Varina Anne. Davis was a loving, indulgent father. Margaret once said, "I wish I could see my father, he would let me be bad." Stories abound of the exploits of the rambunctious Davis children in Richmond during the Civil War. Jeff, Jr., liked to play with a working toy cannon and was a member of a street gang known as the Hill Cats. Joseph, described as his father's hope and joy, was known for interrupting meetings to say bedtime prayers at Davis's knee. A visitor to the Davis house observed, "Statesmen

This photo, taken in 1867, shows four of the six Davis children: from left to right, Jefferson, Jr., Margaret, Varina Anne, and William. Two sons, Samuel and Joseph, died earlier.

passing through the halls on their way to the discussion of weighty things were likely to hear the ringing laughter of the carefree and happy Davis children."

Unfortunately, all of Davis's sons died before him. Samuel died from an unknown disease at age two. Just two weeks after his fifth birthday, Joseph died in an accident when he fell from the porch of the Confederate White House. After the war, 11-year-old William died from diphtheria. And Jeff, Jr., died in a yellow fever epidemic at age 21.

Although both of Davis's daughters survived him, Varina Anne died young. Margaret was the only child to have a family of her own. She married banker Joel Addison Hayes and moved to Colorado Springs, Colorado. Of their five children, four lived to adulthood. Their eldest surviving son changed his name to Hayes-Davis to carry on the Davis family name.

The Statesman Emerges

Jefferson Davis's political philosophy as an adult was deeply rooted in his upbringing and education. At a young age, Davis had been taught the theory of "Jeffersonian democracy," a philosophy based on the thinking of Thomas Jefferson.

Jefferson believed that the rights of the states and their citizens should be protected from violations by the federal government. In the Declaration of Independence, Jefferson wrote that the people have a right to abolish a government that no longer serves their needs. In the mid-1800s, this right would become an important issue for Davis and his fellow Southerners.

Representing Mississippi

Davis's political career began when he was elected to the U.S. House of Representatives from Mississippi in November 1844. He resigned in June 1846 to fight in the U.S.–Mexican War as the leader of a volunteer regiment.

Davis returned home from the war in July 1847 and was appointed to fill a vacant seat for Mississippi in the U.S. Senate. In September 1851, Davis resigned as senator to run for governor of his home state. After his defeat in the November election, Davis settled into life as a private citizen at his plantation, Brierfield.

Jefferson Davis represented Mississippi in the U.S. Congress and later served as secretary of war under President Franklin Pierce.

Davis supervised the huge project of expanding the U.S. Capitol during the 1850s. Wings were added to both sides of the building. The cast-iron dome, approved in 1855, was not completed until 1863, during the Civil War.

Secretary of War

Davis became involved in politics again when he campaigned for his friend Franklin Pierce for president in 1852. Davis had been introduced to Pierce in 1838, while visiting George Wallace Jones, a friend and congressman from the Iowa Territory. After winning the election, Pierce offered Davis the position of secretary of war.

Davis, happy at Brierfield with his second wife and child, was not sure he wanted the job. After much persuasion, however, he accepted, and soon was known as one of the most capable and innovative people ever to hold the title. After all, no one could question his experience. He had been to West Point, had served in the Army in Indian Territory and in the U.S.–Mexican War, and had been chairman of the Senate Committee on Military Affairs.

As secretary of war, Davis improved the military through a series of reforms. Because the United States continued to acquire new territory, the Army was needed more and more to protect the borders and population, especially against the Native Americans. Davis increased the number of men in the Army from approximately 14,000 to more than 18,000. He added four new regiments: two cavalry and two infantry. To encourage men to join and stay in the Army, Davis convinced Congress to approve the first pay raise for the Army in 40 years. He also won support for increases in military pensions and military widow's and orphan's benefits.

Great Improvements

Davis improved the military's weapons and made sure all soldiers knew how to use them. He adopted the rifled musket and the minié ball and experimented with a rifled cannon, repeating firearms, and breech-loading artillery.

Davis felt that a growing country needed a better transportation system to connect the East with the new territories in the West. He sent survey teams to explore possible routes for a transcontinental railroad. The teams also were instructed to study life and lifestyles in those areas, including those of the Native Americans.

As secretary of war, Davis also oversaw building projects handled by the Corps of Engineers. (At this time, the Corps of Engineers oversaw federal construction work in the nation's capital, such as the creation of a water system for the city.) This included the expansion of the U.S. Capitol and the construction of the Washington aqueduct.

Not all of Davis's ideas were well received, however. For instance, he imported camels from Turkey and Egypt to transport Army supplies in the desert climate of the Southwest. Although the camels were effective, they never were accepted by the military and disappeared shortly after Davis left office.

Politics of North and South

When Davis's term as secretary of war ended in 1857, Mississippi again elected him to the U.S. Senate. There were growing concerns among Southerners that federal politics were favoring the North. There was talk of

Key Players

Franklin Pierce
1804–1869

Franklin Pierce became president at a time of growing turmoil. A Northerner from New Hampshire, Pierce's political views nevertheless appealed to Southern voters. He favored states' rights over central government and, therefore, supported slaveholders. Although this position made him unpopular with his abolitionist neighbors, he won the election of 1852, defeating General Winfield Scott, his commanding officer during the U.S.–Mexican War.

As president, Pierce made great economic gains for the country, including the Gadsden Purchase of 1853, which made it possible to build a rail route across the southern portions of present-day California, Arizona, and New Mexico.

However, when Senator Stephen Douglas introduced the Kansas-Nebraska Act in 1854, all previous efforts by Congress to maintain a balance between the interests of slaveholding states and of free states evaporated. President Pierce staunchly defended his pro-slavery Democratic party, a move that pulled at the foundation of national unity. Civil war was on the horizon.

An 1860 cartoon shows Abraham Lincoln winning a baseball game against three other presidential candidates — John Bell, Stephen A. Douglas, and John C. Breckinridge. Lincoln unified the Northern vote, while the others split the Southern vote and lost the election.

secession. Although Davis was a strong supporter of states' rights, he felt that secession should be used only when all else failed.

In the election of 1860, there were four men running for president. The Republicans had Abraham Lincoln. The Democrats split between a Northern candidate, Stephen A. Douglas, and a Southern candidate, John C. Breckinridge, and a third-party candidate, John Bell, also emerged. Davis tried to convince the latter three men to rally around just one candidate instead of dividing the Southern vote. All three remained in the race, however, and Lincoln won the election.

On December 20, 1860, South Carolina became the first state to secede from the Union. On January 21, 1861, Davis announced that Mississippi, too, was seceding. In the four months between Lincoln's election and inauguration, seven Southern states would secede. The start of the Civil War was only three months away.

A Nation Divided

With the election of Abraham Lincoln in 1860, the United States was no longer one nation, indivisible. Statesmen on both sides of the divide, including Jefferson Davis, recognized that the issues that separated the North from the South had been growing for more than 200 years, long before the nation was even formed.

The Invisible Line

The first Africans landed on North American shores in August 1619. Twenty African indentured servants were delivered to the Jamestown (Virginia) colony. As the early colonies grew and plantations spread, a permanent work force was needed to do the backbreaking labor in tobacco, rice, and cotton fields. The North, with smaller farms and more industrial growth, had little need for slaves. Thus, as America grew, an invisible line developed between Northern and Southern ways of life.

In 1819, the territory of Missouri wanted to join the United States as a slaveholding state. At the time, there was an equal number of senators from Northern (free) and Southern (slave) states. Admitting

Since colonial times, when the first Africans were brought to America, slavery was an issue that threatened to divide the nation.

The South built its plantation economy on slave labor. The industrial North did not depend on slavery and considered it immoral. As the country grew, the debate intensified.

a new slave state would tip the balance in the Senate in favor of slavery. In March 1820, the Senate reached what is called the Missouri Compromise: Missouri would enter the Union as a slaveholding state, while Maine would join as a free state. The agreement maintained the delicate balance between slave and free states. It also created a line that extended westward from Missouri's southern border, above which all new states would be free.

Tariffs That Hurt the South

By the 1830s, the United States, led by the industrial North, had imposed a series of tariffs on imported merchandise. These tariffs, or taxes, made it more expensive for Americans to buy European-manufactured goods. But the less Americans bought from abroad,

Senators Daniel Webster of Massachusetts (left) and Henry Clay of Kentucky (center) pushed for the Compromise of 1850, which limited the expansion of slavery in new states. John C. Calhoun, the senator from South Carolina (right), believed that each state had a right to allow or ban slavery as it saw fit.

the fewer raw materials European manufacturers would purchase from Southern plantations. Vice President John C. Calhoun, a believer in states' rights, came up with an idea to combat the tariffs. He said that any state could declare a federal law invalid if the state did not agree with it. Calhoun's idea, called *nullification*, met with opposition from both the North and the South.

Even Davis disagreed with nullification as a solution to the issue of tariffs. When there was a chance that he would be transferred to South Carolina to enforce the collection of tariffs, Davis decided he would rather resign from the Army than march against South Carolina. Eventually, a compromise was reached. The tariff would be gradually lowered over a 10-year period. But the split between North and South widened.

New States, New Conflicts

As more Americans moved west, more territories sought to become states. When the vast area west of Iowa and Missouri wanted to join the Union, a law was passed splitting it into two states, Kansas and

Westward expansion and emigration during the mid-19th century fed the political debate raging between the North and the South. With the establishment of each new state, the nation came closer to splitting in two.

Nebraska. But would these states be slave or free? Since they were above the Missouri Compromise line, which required new states to be free, it seemed that the matter was settled. But the law, called the Kansas-Nebraska Act, stated that the people living in those states should decide the question of slavery. Northern states were outraged, for this voided the Missouri Compromise. Soon the race was on for control of the new states. The phrase "bleeding Kansas" began to describe the terrible bloodshed that exploded as proslavery and antislavery groups clashed.

By 1860, Southerners felt that the federal government no longer served the needs of their states. The South saw its way of life slipping away. The election of Abraham Lincoln as president in November was the final blow. By February 1861, seven Southern states had seceded from the Union, and Davis had been chosen president of the Confederacy.

Secession!

The Tenth Amendment to the U.S. Constitution, adopted in 1791, states that "the powers not delegated to the United States by the Constitution, nor prohibited by it to the States, are reserved to the States respectively, or to the people." That is a formal way of saying that the individual states have the right to do anything not specifically granted to the federal government by the Constitution.

A political cartoon from the 1860s characterizes the fight between the South (Secession) and the North (Union). Two men representing Britain and France stand by with clubs to re-arm the South, a possibility of great concern to the North.

It does seem rather simple. With this amendment, the Founding Fathers intended to protect American citizens from a too-powerful federal government. But over the years, some people interpreted the Tenth Amendment to suit their own purposes.

John C. Calhoun was a Democrat from South Carolina and vice president under presidents John Quincy Adams and Andrew Jackson. Early in his political career, Calhoun favored national interests over those of the individual states. But by 1828, he had become angry about the effect of tariffs on the economy of his home state. Making a complete turnaround, Calhoun began promoting the rights of the states over those of the federal government. His doctrine of nullification said that a state could ignore a federal law with which it disagreed. Taken to its extreme conclusion, nullification implied that a state could even leave the Union if its differences with the national government became too great.

The argument for states' rights led to the secession of the Southern states in an effort to preserve their right to own slaves. And yet the new nation, the Confederate States of America, ultimately was doomed by the same claim. Using states' rights as their motto, many in the South refused to cooperate with President Jefferson Davis as he tried to form the individual Confederate states into a cohesive whole capable of fighting the Union army.

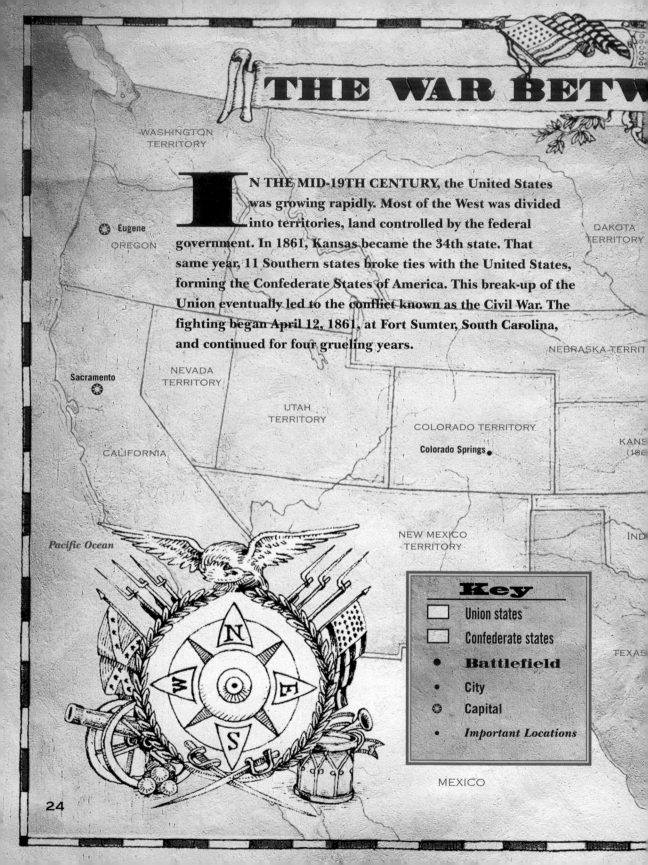

WASHINGTON
TERRITORY

DAKOTA
TERRITORY

⊛ Eugene
OREGON

I N THE MID-19TH CENTURY, the United States
was growing rapidly. Most of the West was divided
into territories, land controlled by the federal
government. In 1861, Kansas became the 34th state. That
same year, 11 Southern states broke ties with the United States,
forming the Confederate States of America. This break-up of the
Union eventually led to the conflict known as the Civil War. The
fighting began April 12, 1861, at Fort Sumter, South Carolina,
and continued for four grueling years.

NEBRASKA TERRIT

Sacramento
⊛

NEVADA
TERRITORY

UTAH
TERRITORY

COLORADO TERRITORY

KANS
(186

Colorado Springs •

CALIFORNIA

NEW MEXICO
TERRITORY

IND

Pacific Ocean

Key

☐ Union states

☐ Confederate states

• **Battlefield**

• City

⊛ Capital

• *Important Locations*

TEXAS

MEXICO

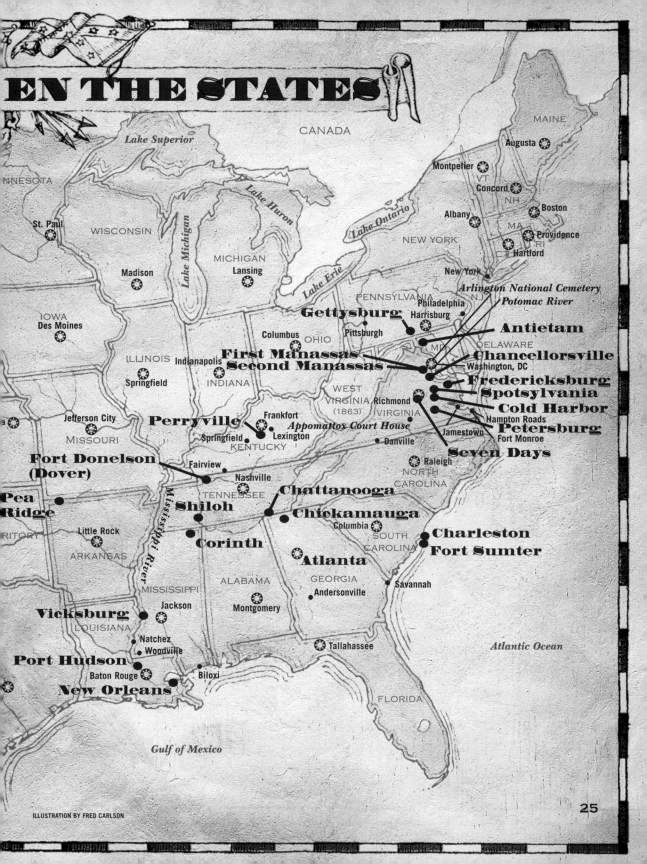

EN THE STATES

ILLUSTRATION BY FRED CARLSON

25

The Confederate President

Was Davis Doomed to Defeat?

In February 1861, Jefferson Davis was tending his garden with his wife, Varina, when he looked up to see a lone rider galloping at full speed toward the Davis plantation, Brierfield. Reining his horse to a quick stop, the rider leaned over and handed Davis a telegram.

"Sir: We are directed to inform you that you are this day unanimously elected President of the Provisional Government of the Confederate States of America and to request you to come to Montgomery [Alabama] immediately."

Fast Fact

In 1861, the Confederate states had a population of approximately

9.1 million

compared with Union states with

22.3 million.

Leading a New Nation

Jefferson Davis had not attended the Montgomery convention that had approved a provisional constitution for the Confederate States of America. But the political leaders who did attend — from Georgia, Florida, South Carolina, Alabama, Louisiana, and Mississippi — had unanimously elected him president of the Confederacy. "I was surprised, and, still more, disappointed," Davis recalled years later.

Davis had hoped for a military role. Moreover, he felt certain a long, bloody war with the Union was coming soon. "We are without machinery, without means, and threatened by a powerful opposition," he wrote his wife, Varina, "but I do not despond, and will not shrink from the task imposed upon me."

Davis did not want to see the United States split apart. He even sent a peace commission to Washington, D.C., to try to prevent war. But the rift between North and South had grown too large.

On February 18, 1861, a band played "Dixie" as Davis mounted the steps of the state capitol in Montgomery, Alabama, to give his inaugural address. He concluded his speech by saying, "We may hopefully look forward to success, to peace, and to prosperity."

Davis took the oath as president of the Confederate States of America at the Alabama state capitol in Montgomery. In his inaugural address, he compared the Confederates to the patriots who had fought for independence in the Revolutionary War.

Despite these stirring words, however, the next four years would spell the end of all three for Davis and the new nation he led.

Constitution and Cabinet

The constitution of the Confederate States of America, under which Davis governed, was based on the U.S. Constitution. Additional clauses emphasized states' rights and allowed for amendments to be passed by only two-thirds of the states. The constitution forbade laws impairing slaveholders' property rights and the importation of slaves from any foreign country, and limited the president to a single term of six years.

Davis divided his Cabinet positions among men from different states. Alexander H. Stephens from Georgia was vice president.

Alexander H. Stephens
(1812–1883)

Alexander H. Stephens of Georgia was a member of the U.S. House of Representatives during the debates over states' rights and the crafting of the Compromise of 1850 that attempted to balance Southern and Northern interests. Although he did not favor secession, he defended the rights of slaveholders. When lines were drawn between Unionists and Secessionists, Stephens reluctantly sided with the South and accepted the office of vice president of the Confederacy with mixed feelings.

In public, Stephens was the loyal vice president of the Confederacy. In private, he criticized Davis as "weak and vacillating, timid, petulant, peevish, and obstinate." In February 1865, Davis sent Stephens to Hampton Roads, Virginia, to negotiate terms of peace with the North, a mission that proved unsuccessful.

After the Civil War, Stephens continued to represent Georgia in the House of Representatives and later as governor.

Robert Toombs, also of Georgia, became secretary of state. Christopher Memminger of South Carolina became secretary of the treasury. Alabama's Leroy P. Walker and Florida's Stephen Mallory headed the war and navy departments, respectively. Texas's John H. Reagan was postmaster general, and Louisiana's Judah P. Benjamin became attorney general. Of all the Cabinet members, only Benjamin was Davis's personal friend.

Davis enjoyed tremendous popularity among the Southern people during the first year of the Confederacy. But he quickly clashed with members of his Cabinet. He often demanded too many details from the state and war departments, for example, as if he wanted to make all important decisions himself. Toombs and Walker left their positions after a few months.

Davis also lacked tact. He often was abrupt and irritable toward colleagues. He rarely entertained or took other steps to build goodwill. Davis's wife, Varina, later commented, "He did not know the arts of the politician."

Davis could not handle criticism and felt he was misunderstood. "I wish I could learn just to let people alone who snap at me," Davis admitted to his wife.

Unfortunately, Davis's quickness to take offense made him a difficult man with whom to work. During the four-year life of the Confederacy, Davis appointed 14 men to the seven Cabinet positions. At the end, only Benjamin, Mallory, and Reagan remained from the original Cabinet.

A No-Win Situation

In addition, favoritism weakened Davis's management of the military. Among his generals, Davis respected Robert E. Lee, Albert Johnston, Braxton Bragg, and J.C. Pemberton. However, he often criticized other high-ranking officers, including Pierre G.T. Beauregard and Joseph E. Johnston.

By 1862, it became clear the Civil War would be long and bloody. Davis's general popularity began to decline. After military setbacks, newspapers such as the *Charleston Mercury* and the *Daily Richmond Examiner* relentlessly criticized Davis.

Davis was in a no-win situation. The North was urban and industrialized. It could manufacture most of its own weapons. The rural South's only commodity was cotton. And, the Union's naval blockade kept the South from shipping enough cotton to Europe to establish credit and buy sufficient supplies.

The Confederate treasury tried to raise money with bonds and high taxes. Both measures were unpopular, and the paper money issued by the treasury was almost worthless. Moreover, the states that had fought so hard for states' rights resisted Davis's efforts to create a strong, central government for the Confederacy.

Key Players

Judah P. Benjamin
(1811–1884)

Before the Civil War, Judah P. Benjamin, a prominent lawyer in Louisiana, served three terms in the U.S. Senate. It was rumored that he once challenged Davis to a duel because of a perceived insult. After Davis publicly apologized, however, the two became great friends. He served as Davis's first attorney general. Later, he became secretary of war and then secretary of state. Many Northerners considered him "the brains of the Confederacy."

With the fall of the Confederate States of America in 1865, Benjamin fled to the West Indies and then to England, where he resumed life as a lawyer. He never returned to the United States.

The First Military Draft

Throughout the Civil War, the army of the North outnumbered that of the South. Without enough volunteers, Davis's administration started the first military draft in American history. It proved highly unpopular. Even Vice President Stephens complained that mandatory enrollment in the military was unconstitutional. The draft pulled men away from their farms, causing severe food shortages. Soldiers often were underfed and ill-equipped.

Citizens at home went hungry, too. "Bread riots" broke out in Richmond, Atlanta, and other Southern cities. Secretary of War James A. Seddon finally agreed in late 1863 to let government supplies help feed poor civilians, but there still was not enough food.

With each bloody battle, the death toll mounted. After the Battle of Antietam, President Abraham Lincoln issued the Emancipation Proclamation, which made slavery a moral issue in the war. That kept England and France from assisting the South. It also slowly allowed black troops to be organized to fight for the North. City after city fell in the South during 1863 and 1864. The Confederacy was losing the war.

As the war dragged on, Southern funds and supplies ran low and volunteers were few. In an attempt to fool the Union army into thinking the South was strong, the Confederates set up decoys in place of real soldiers and guns.

Retreat and Surrender

In early 1865, Davis sent men to Hampton Roads, Virginia, to negotiate with the North. The North wanted peace, but it would never recognize the Confederacy as a separate nation. Forever dedicated to the concept of states' rights, Davis kept fighting. Still hoping for a victory, the Confederate Congress passed a bill permitting slaves to enlist. Any slave who enlisted would be free.

As Federal troops prepared to invade Richmond in April 1865, Davis and the Confederate government abandoned the capital and fled to Danville, Virginia. Davis wept when he learned about General Robert E. Lee's surrender to General Ulysses S. Grant at Appomattox Court House, Virginia, on April 9.

Davis began his presidency promising to maintain the Southern states' "right to self-government at all hazards." He never gave up, but the North won the Civil War nonetheless.

Raiders, Cruisers, and Blockade Runners

A showdown between the Union warship *Kearsarge* (left) and the Confederate raider *Alabama* (right) took place off the coast of France on June 19, 1864. The duel, witnessed by thousands from shore, ended with the sinking of the Confederate ship.

When the Civil War began in 1861, the South had no formal navy and no real means of building warships. But that did not prevent it from making the North feel its naval sting.

When the Union's navy moved into place to begin a blockade of the entire Southern coastline in April 1861, the Confederacy knew it could not allow itself to be choked off from contact with the rest of the world. The South depended upon open waters to export its cotton and tobacco. It also needed access to the sea in order to import guns and ammunition.

The *Kearsarge* had an experienced crew and a surprise: reinforced iron sides that the *Alabama* could barely dent. The *Alabama* (in the distance) was unable to withstand the barrage of Union cannonfire, and the crew was forced to abandon the sinking ship.

Privateers and Blockade Runners

The Confederate government proposed several plans to oppose the North on the waterways. Confederate president Jefferson Davis pleaded with all Southern ship owners to volunteer on the side of the South. These privately owned ships, or privateers, could obtain letters of marque and capture merchant ships at sea. Early in the war, a few privateers harassed and took over Union merchant ships, which led Northern newspapers to publish stories about damages inflicted by these vessels.

More important were blockade runners — Confederate ships that tried to "run," or slip through, the Union blockade. These swift, light vessels could venture into shallow waters, slip between the blockade ships, and outsail many of them. Blockade runners loaded with cotton headed for Bermuda or the Bahamas in the Atlantic Ocean, where they sold their cargo and loaded up with supplies for the Confederate troops.

Blockade runners employed various tricks to get past Union ships. They usually would wait for a moonless night to slip in and out of Southern ports. The vessels often were painted a dull color to conceal them in darkness. And smokeless coal was used to power the engines, with the steam released underwater. Some blockade runners even hugged the shoreline, where the sound of incoming waves overpowered the engine noise.

Blockade running was extremely profitable. Cotton could be bought in the South for six cents per pound and sold for many times that amount in England. One Confederate ship, the *Robert E. Lee*, reportedly ran the Union blockade more than 20 times, delivering more than 6,000 bales of cotton (worth about two million dollars in gold). But eventually, the Union blockade became more effective, and more and more Confederate runners were captured.

> Commerce raiders, or cruisers, were designed with one purpose in mind: to wreak havoc on Union merchant ships.

Captured by Raiders

In addition to the privately owned blockade runners, the South depended heavily on commerce raiders, which used Confederate navy ships. Commerce raiders, or cruisers, were designed with one purpose in mind: to wreak havoc on Union merchant ships. More than a dozen of these armed vessels from the South were equipped with both engines and sails and usually displayed a flag other than that of the Confederacy in order to deceive Union ships. Once captured, a Union ship's cargo would be seized, the crew or passengers taken aboard the cruiser, and the captured ship burned.

However, it was necessary sometimes to release a Union ship if the cruiser could not accommodate the number of crewmembers from the captured vessel. Released on "ransom bond" (based on the value of the cargo), the captain had to agree to pay the Confederacy a certain amount of money at a future date.

Commerce raiders were very effective in damaging Union shipping. CSS *Florida* captured 23 ships in just seven months (one captured ship and its cargo alone were worth two million dollars).

Fast Fact

The Union blockade consisted of

500

ships monitoring

3,500

miles of Southern coastline, including

12

major ports.

And CSS *Shenandoah* disrupted the Yankee whaling fleet in the North Pacific Ocean.

Duel at Sea

Perhaps the most famous commerce raider was CSS *Alabama*, captained by Raphael Semmes. This cruiser captured grain, whaling, and other merchant ships. In two years, the *Alabama* destroyed more than 60 Union ships, worth approximately six million dollars. The *Alabama*'s career came to an end, however, in June 1864, when it was discovered off the coast of Cherbourg, France. John Winslow, captain of the Union warship *Kearsarge*, was determined to stop Semmes from inflicting any more damage on the high seas. Semmes challenged Winslow to a ship-to-ship duel on June 19.

Cotton, tobacco, and other exports await shipment at the port of New Orleans. One of the Union's first strategic moves was to choke the South's ability to finance its war effort by preventing exports from reaching Europe.

Thousands of onlookers watched from the shore and from nearby boats. Several miles off the coast of France, the two ships repeatedly circled each other — about 500 yards apart — while firing. Many of the *Alabama*'s shots did not appear to damage the *Kearsarge*. Semmes did not know the *Kearsarge* was well protected by heavy chains, concealed by planks, that covered her sides. He later claimed that the *Alabama* did not stand a chance against this ironclad.

In addition, the gunners on the *Kearsarge* were much more experienced than those on the *Alabama*. Semmes and his crew held off as long as they could before abandoning their sinking ship. Shortly after jumping into the sea, Semmes was rescued by a British yacht, enabling him to avoid capture by the *Kearsarge*.

The Confederacy proved to be quite resourceful in challenging the Union navy for as long as it did. Commerce raiding alone caused marine insurance to increase more than 900 percent. It took the North years to recover financially.

A Spy in the Confederate White House

This is a fictional account of Mary Elizabeth Bowser's role as a Union spy. Although some facts are known about her early life, very little is truly known about her later years. We know that Bowser was a real person who, before gaining her freedom, served as a slave in the Van Lew home. The story associated with her is that she was placed as a Union spy in the Confederate White House in Richmond. But mystery surrounds Bowser's story. Before her death in 1900, Bowser's former mistress, Elizabeth Van Lew, who was a Union supporter during the Civil War, requested that the U.S. War Department return her correspondence, which she then destroyed. In 1904, the diary of Thomas McNiven, one of Mary's supposed contacts, was destroyed by his executor. Although it is impossible to confirm that Mary was indeed a spy, it is fascinating to imagine what it might have been like to be...a spy in the Confederate White House.

President Jefferson Davis never suspected Mary Bowser of being a Union spy.

As Mary went about her daily chores, she kept her ears open. Little did President Jefferson Davis know that he had a Union spy in his own household serving his guests. This black servant, who Davis assumed was illiterate, was really a valuable Union army spy. She was a member of Elizabeth Van Lew's "Richmond Underground" spy network. Born around 1836 in Virginia on a plantation owned by John Van Lew, Mary served John and his daughter, Elizabeth. As a child, she worked in the house serving and cleaning. When John Van Lew died in 1851, Elizabeth, a secret abolitionist, freed all of the family slaves. Since they were treated fairly, the freed slaves chose to stay on at the plantation. As the years passed, Mary began to show an aptitude for learning. Elizabeth, who had been educated by Quakers in Philadelphia, sent Mary to school there.

Mary kept up a pretense of being simple in order to learn Confederate secrets.

Eyes and Ears Open

By 1861 and the start of the Civil War, Mary was married and living again in Richmond, Virginia. Her former mistress, Elizabeth Van Lew, had established a spy ring serving the Union. She asked Mary to work with her. Using her social position in Richmond, Elizabeth helped place Mary as a servant in the Confederate White House around 1863.

Davis never knew how bright or educated Mary was. Mary kept up a pretense of being simple in order to learn Confederate secrets. In the course of going about her household chores, Mary kept her eyes and ears open for any valuable information. Perhaps she scanned the papers on Davis's desk as she pretended to dust, memorizing anything she thought important. These items might have included lists of troop movements, battle plans, treasury reports, and reports on the movement of Union prisoners.

Mary then passed the information to Van Lew or to Thomas McNiven. McNiven was the main Union undercover agent in Richmond. He ran a bakery that served as an exchange point for intelligence information. Whenever he delivered bakery products to the Davis home, Mary would try to pass along any valuable information. Even at the end of the Civil War, Davis never realized that his seemingly faithful servant was a Union spy.

The date and place of Mary Elizabeth Bowser's death are unknown. In 1995, however, she was inducted into the U.S. Military Intelligence Corps Hall of Fame at Fort Huachuca, Arizona, honoring her for courage on a dangerous mission.

Fast Fact

On February 9, 1864, Elizabeth Van Lew helped

109

Union soldiers escape from Richmond's Libby Prison.

The Confederate Image

Art of the Civil War South

The Civil War was a grueling experience for most Southerners — not only for the tens of thousands of soldiers who were wounded or killed in battle, but also for the women, children, elderly, and infirm left behind to care for their homes and families. As the war dragged on, they suffered widespread shortages of food and other vital supplies. Even paper supplies dwindled, forcing several newspapers to print the news on wallpaper.

It is difficult to imagine that in this atmosphere of desperation, Southerners could maintain their love for art, but they did. Unfortunately, however, supplies of art and the materials needed to produce it, like supplies of bread and sugar, grew increasingly scarce.

Cherished Pictures

Such shortages were not evident at the start of the conflict. In early 1861, the Confederacy won the first battle of the war at Manassas, also called Bull Run, in northern Virginia. During the battle, the president of the Confederate States of America, Jefferson Davis, rode out from the capital of Richmond to observe his troops in action. In the flush of victory, reports reached home that Davis had taken to the field in uniform and had actually led the army. The story was untrue, but within weeks, artists had produced pictures showing Davis as a general on horseback at "Bull's Run."

In the era before newspapers could print photographs, "prints" were cherished display pieces for family parlors. Pictures were drawn with a special crayon on a slab of stone (lithographs) or carved with a sharp tool onto a steel plate (engravings), then printed by the hundreds on durable, heavy paper.

For a variety of reasons, Southern printmakers virtually ceased issuing pictures for the home within a year after First Manassas. In fact, not until the war was over did Southerners finally get to see

The Confederate victory at the Battle of First Manassas inspired this print of Confederate president Jefferson Davis in full military uniform. Rumors that he actually led the Southern army were false.

and own pictures of their most beloved hero, General Robert E. Lee. Incredibly, not one print of Lee was published while the Confederacy was still alive.

Deprived of Art

Why did Confederate printmaking decline so swiftly? Chronic shortages of ink and paper were part of the reason, but the shortage of manpower was the main cause of the decline. Many artists were drafted into the army, and those who were spared were ordered to focus on a different kind of printmaking. The new government needed postage stamps and money, and artists who had created large portraits to hang above family fireplaces now created tiny ones to grace dollar bills and penny stamps.

Baltimore and New Orleans, two Southern cities where art flourished, were soon deprived of their artistic influence. Baltimore was cut off from the Confederacy when Maryland chose to remain in the Union, and local artists with Southern sympathies were forced to abandon Confederate printmaking or work in secret. In New Orleans, opportunities were no greater. The city was captured by the Union army early in the war, and from that point on, artistic "disloyalty" was not tolerated. When one local painter was caught working on a portrait of Confederate general Thomas "Stonewall" Jackson, he was arrested.

A Sentimental Masterpiece

One notable exception to the shortage of art was a painting titled *The Burial of Latane*. When a Richmond artist named William D. Washington heard the story of a Confederate cavalry officer killed in a skirmish outside the city in 1862, he could not help but capitalize on the situation. The victim had been denied a formal funeral when Union troops surrounding the plantation to which the body had been carted refused to allow a minister to pass through the lines. Undaunted, the women and black slaves of the plantation buried the officer. Washington painted a sentimental scene of these full-skirted women in prayer, suggesting the courage and

Paper and ink were in short supply, so artists turned their talents to practical tasks such as printing Confederate dollar bills and postage stamps. Below: After the war, Virginians sold copies of a print published in New York to raise funds for a commemorative statue of Robert E. Lee.

sacrifices of Southern women and perpetuating the myth of the steadfast loyalty of the slaves.

The painting was a sensation in Richmond. Wherever it was displayed, an empty pail was set beneath it so Southerners could donate money to care for the war wounded. Because Southern print-makers were no longer able to copy paintings for mass distribution, however, the work remained virtually unknown throughout the South until after the war.

Despite its popularity, *The Burial of Latane*, a painting that aroused Confederate sympathy, was not available as a print until after the war. Those who could afford the expensive print had to purchase it from a New York printer.

Northern Printmakers

Following the war, Northern engravers and lithographers entered the Southern market, taking up where the ravaged Southern picture industry had left off. By 1868, a New York publisher was selling engravings of *The Burial of Latane* for the then-hefty sum of 20 dollars apiece. Not long afterward, when Virginians organized an effort to build a statue of Lee in Richmond, they too hired a New Yorker to engrave a print that could be sold to raise funds for the project. And the fierce "Stonewall" Jackson, seen in wartime only in British-made prints showing him without his famous beard, became immortalized in prints made in New York, Philadelphia, and Boston. Even Jefferson Davis, whom many Southerners blamed for the defeat of the Confederacy, enjoyed a comeback in the 1870s and 1880s, thanks in part to a series of prints that portrayed him as a hero.

Thus, much of what we identify as the Confederate image was a product not of the South, but of its bitter enemy, the North. The Confederate "cause" had been ill-served by its artists, through no fault of their own, but the "lost cause" would be romanticized in dozens of prints made, ironically, in the North.

Symbol of the Lost Cause

Following the fall of the Confederate capital, Richmond, Virginia, and the surrender of General Robert E. Lee's army in April 1865, Jefferson Davis and a small group of government officials and followers fled the state. They went to North Carolina, South Carolina, and then on to Georgia. Davis hoped to continue the struggle by eventually reaching Confederate forces in the West.

Prisoner at Fort Monroe

At dawn on May 10, 1865, Davis and his family were captured by Federal cavalry near Irwinville, Georgia. Taken to Savannah, they were placed aboard a ship that took them to Fort Monroe in Virginia.

Davis was imprisoned at Fort Monroe for almost two years. For about one week, he even had a ball and chain restraint on his leg, but this was removed due to public outcry. For three months, Davis was allowed no contact with his family. One soldier remained in his cell at all times, while more soldiers walked constantly outside the door. The light inside Davis's cell was never permitted to be out. He became quite ill during his imprisonment, and never fully recovered his health. On May 3, 1866, almost a year after he was captured, Davis's wife, Varina, was allowed to visit for the first time.

Jefferson Davis was held in Virginia's Fort Monroe for almost two years. He suffered a significant decline in health and vitality. In 1867, Davis reentered society old beyond his years.

Freedom and a New Life

Varina worked tirelessly for her husband's release and sought the help of prominent Northerners. On May 13, 1867, Davis left prison on a $100,000 bond provided by a group of supporters, including the famous Northern newspaperman Horace Greeley. The U.S. government never brought Davis to trial on any charge.

After his release, Davis traveled throughout the United States, Canada, and Europe. In November 1869, he accepted a job as president of the Carolina Life Insurance Company. The company struggled and did not achieve great success. In the economic panic of 1873, the company went under and Davis lost all his money. He also was offered the position of senator from Mississippi in 1875, but he turned it down. Before he could have returned to the Senate, Davis would have had to request a pardon. He refused to do this, stating that it would look as though he were admitting that what the South had done had been a mistake. Davis did not feel that his actions were wrong. He believed that maintaining the dignity of the office he had held was more important than recovering his financial fortunes. As a result, Davis's family lived in reduced circumstances for most of the rest of his life.

Beauvoir

In 1877, a piece of good luck came Davis's way. An admirer named Sarah Dorsey rented a cottage on the grounds of her home, Beauvoir (meaning "beautiful view"), located near Biloxi, Mississippi, to Davis. There, he enjoyed the view of the Gulf of Mexico while working on his memoirs. Davis's

At Beauvoir, near Biloxi, Mississippi, Davis wrote his memoirs and enjoyed a quiet life. Although he supported the government's Reconstruction efforts, Davis never asked to have his citizenship reinstated.

More than 200,000 mourners attended Davis's funeral in New Orleans. It was the largest funeral for any American until President John F. Kennedy's in 1963.

two-volume book, *The Rise and Fall of the Confederate Government*, was published in 1881. Dorsey arranged to sell Beauvoir to Davis for $5,500. He made the first house payment before Dorsey's death in 1879. Davis then found she had left the entire estate to him in her will.

In his last years, Davis left Beauvoir from time to time, traveling through parts of the South, visiting friends and acquaintances, and making occasional speeches. He did not involve himself in the politics of the day, but he did enjoy seeing veterans of the Civil War and their families. Although not bitter, he also never apologized. And, Davis never sought to have his citizenship reinstated. In his public remarks, Davis encouraged other Southerners to focus on giving their best efforts toward helping America grow and prosper.

On December 6, 1889, while on a business trip, Davis died suddenly — most likely of pneumonia — in New Orleans, Louisiana. His funeral in New Orleans attracted more than 200,000 mourners. Buried originally in New Orleans, Davis's body was brought to Hollywood Cemetery in Richmond, Virginia, in 1893.

In 1903, Varina sold Beauvoir to the Mississippi Division of the United Sons of Confederate Veterans. She asked that the property be used as a soldiers' home, and after that, as a museum to the memory of Davis and the Confederate soldiers.

In 1978, President Jimmy Carter approved a joint congressional resolution that posthumously restored full rights of citizenship to Davis. When introducing the resolution, Senator Mark Hatfield of Oregon stated that "with this resolution I seek to keep his memory green and restore the rights due to an outstanding American."

'Daughter of the Confederacy'

The last of the six Davis children, Varina Anne, was born on June 27, 1864, just nine months before Richmond, Virginia, fell to the Union army. She was the only one of Jefferson Davis's children allowed to visit him when he was imprisoned at Fort Monroe in Virginia. Davis felt the older children would have a difficult time with his situation, but young Varina Anne, or Winnie, became his comfort and amusement. Their close relationship continued as Winnie grew older.

After being educated in Europe, 17-year-old Winnie returned to Mississippi to be with her parents. She was her father's companion during his last years at Beauvoir. They took walks along the beach, discussed literature, and played cards. When Davis was asked to speak at Confederate ceremonies, Winnie went with him.

At a gathering in Atlanta, Georgia, in 1886, Winnie was introduced as the "Daughter of the Confederacy." Loved by veterans, she became a new Southern symbol. Unfortunately, the public attention had tragic effects. When Winnie became engaged to attorney Alfred Wilkenson, the Davis family received threatening letters. Wilkenson was a Northerner and the grandson of a noted abolitionist. Winnie was torn between her role as Davis's daughter and her love for Wilkenson. The stress increased when Winnie, traveling in Europe, received word that Davis had died. Feeling it her duty to carry on in her father's place, Winnie broke off the engagement. She never married.

Winnie spent her last years with her mother in New York City. She wrote magazine and newspaper articles and two novels. She continued to attend Confederate ceremonies. While attending a Confederate reunion in July 1898, Winnie became ill. Six weeks later, she died at age 34 from complications arising from what was thought to be malaria.

CIVIL WAR

1860

NOV 6
Abraham Lincoln is elected 16th president of the United States.

Lincoln

1861

FEB 9
Formation of the Confederate States of America (CSA) by secessionist states South Carolina, Mississippi, Florida, Alabama, Georgia, Louisiana, and Texas. Jefferson Davis elected CSA president.

Davis

MAR 4
Lincoln's inauguration

APR 12
Fort Sumter (South Carolina) Civil War begins with Confederate attack under Gen. Pierre Beauregard.

APR 15
Lincoln issues proclamation calling for 75,000 troops. Gen. Winfield Scott becomes commander of Union army.

APR 17
Virginia joins CSA, followed by Arkansas, Tennessee, and North Carolina.

APR 20
Gen. Robert E. Lee resigns from U.S. Army and accepts command in Confederate army.

JUL 21
First Manassas (Virginia) Gen. Thomas J. "Stonewall" Jackson defeats Gen. Irvin McDowell.

NOV 1
Gen. George B. McClellan assumes command of Union forces.

1862

FEB 11-16
Fort Donelson (Tennessee) Gen. Ulysses S. Grant breaks major Confederate stronghold.

MAR
McClellan begins Peninsular Campaign, heading to Richmond, Virginia, the Confederate capital.

APR 6-7
Shiloh (Tennessee) Grant defeats Beauregard and Gen. A.S. Johnston. Heavy losses on both sides.

APR 24

New Orleans (Louisiana) Gen. David Farragut leads 17 Union gunboats up Mississippi River and takes New Orleans, the South's most important seaport.

JUN 25-JUL 1
Seven Days (Virginia) Six major battles are fought over seven days near Richmond, Virginia. Lee is victorious, protecting the Confederate capital from Union occupation.

Halleck

JUL 18
Lincoln turns over command to Gen. Henry W. Halleck.

AUG 29-30
Second Manassas (Virginia) Jackson and Gen. James Longstreet defeat Gen. John Pope.

SEP 17
Antietam (Maryland) McClellan narrowly defeats Lee. Bloodiest day in American military history: 23,000 casualties.

SEP 22

Lincoln issues preliminary Emancipation Proclamation, freeing slaves in Confederate states.

OCT 3-4
Corinth (Mississippi) Gen. William Rosecrans defeats Gen. Earl Van Dorn.

44

NOTE: Battles are in black type, with flags indicating: Union victory ▬ Confederate victory ▨

TIME LINE

NOV 7
Lincoln replaces McClellan with Gen. Ambrose Burnside to lead Army of the Potomac.

Burnside

DEC 13
Fredericksburg (Virginia) Lee defeats Burnside.

1863

JAN 1
Final Emancipation Proclamation frees slaves in Confederate states. Union army begins enlisting black soldiers.

JAN 25
Lincoln replaces Burnside with Gen. Joseph Hooker.

Hooker

JAN 29
Grant is placed in command of the Union army in the West.

MAY 1-4
Chancellorsville (Virginia) Lee defeats Hooker.

JUN 28
Lincoln replaces Hooker with Gen. George E. Meade.

JUL 1-3

Gettysburg (Pennsylvania) Meade defeats Lee.

JUL 4
Vicksburg (Mississippi) After weeks of seige, Grant takes the Confederate stronghold on Mississippi River, effectively dividing eastern and western Confederate forces.

SEP 18-20
Chickamauga (Georgia) Gen. Braxton Bragg defeats Rosecrans.

OCT 16
Lincoln puts Grant in charge of all western operations.

NOV 19
Lincoln delivers the Gettysburg Address, dedicating the battlefield as a national cemetery.

NOV 23-25
Chattanooga (Tennessee) Grant defeats Bragg.

1864

MAR 9
Lincoln puts Grant in command of entire Union army. Gen. William T. Sherman takes over western operations.

MAY 8-21
Spotsylvania (Virginia) Grant defeats Lee.

MAY 31-JUN 12
Cold Harbor (Virginia) Lee defeats Grant and Meade.

JUN 15-18

Petersburg (Virginia) Lee and Beauregard defeat Grant and Meade.

NOV 8
Lincoln is re-elected.

NOV 15-DEC 21

Sherman's "March to the Sea." Sherman destroys supplies and transportation systems from Atlanta to Savannah (Georgia), crippling the Confederacy.

Lee

1865

APR 2
Petersburg (Virginia) Grant defeats Lee. Confederates leave Richmond.

APR 9
Lee surrenders to Grant at Appomattox Court House, Virginia.

APR 14
Lincoln is shot by John Wilkes Booth at Ford's Theatre, Washington, D.C. He dies the following morning.

DEC 6
Thirteenth Amendment to the Constitution abolishing slavery is ratified.

GRAPHICS BY FRED CARLSON

45

Glossary

Abolish: To get rid of completely. An *abolitionist* works to end slavery.

Amendment: An addition or alteration to a document. The U.S. Constitution currently has 27 Amendments.

Aptitude: Ability and quickness in learning.

Aqueduct: A bridge-like structure that supports a canal passing over low ground.

Boarding school: A school where students receive meals and lodging, along with an education.

Breech-loading: A firearm that is designed to be loaded behind the barrel.

Cabinet: In government, the official advisors to the president (or other head of state); the people appointed to executive positions, such as secretary of state, secretary of war, etc.

Commodity: Something that can be traded.

Confederacy: In the American Civil War, the alliance of states that broke ties with the U.S. government to form a new government, called the Confederate States of America. The states that did not secede supported the Union.

Constitution: The basic set of laws that define a government and guide its decisions and direction.

Diphtheria: A disease that causes a high fever, difficulty breathing, and weakness.

Dominican friars: Members of a religious order established in 1216 by St. Dominic.

Emancipation: Freedom from slavery or other form of bondage.

Executor: In legal terms, the person responsible for honoring the "last will and testament" of a deceased person.

Exemplary: Worthy of imitation.

Export: To send or transport goods or materials to a foreign country for trade or sale.

Headmaster: The man who is principal of a (usually) private school. A female principal of such a school is called a *headmistress*.

Import: To bring or carry in goods or materials from a foreign country for trade or sale.

Inauguration: The formal beginning of a term in office.

Indentured: Bound by contract into service for another.

Letters of marque: Documents issued by a nation that allowed private citizens to equip their ships with arms and seize citizens or goods of another nation.

Malaria: An infectious disease passed by a species of mosquito, causing chills, fever, and sweating.

Minié ball: A cone-shaped rifle bullet with a hollow base that expands when fired.

Nullification: The refusal or failure of a U.S. state to recognize or enforce a federal law within its boundaries.

Plantation: A large estate, often with resident workers, that produces income crops.

Posthumously: Occurring after one's death.

Secede: To make a formal withdrawal from an organization, alliance, or, in American history, a nation. Secession occurred when 11 states officially withdrew from the United States of America and formed a new nation, the Confederate States of America.

Tact: Sensitivity as to what is proper and appropriate when dealing with others.

Tariffs: Taxes imposed by a government on goods coming into or going out of a country.

Union: In the American Civil War, the states that supported the United States government. The states that did not support the U.S. seceded to form the Confederate States of America.

Yellow fever: An infectious disease passed by certain tropical mosquitoes, causing high fever, jaundice, and vomiting.

Index

Alabama (Confederate ship): 31, 34
Ampudia, Pedro de: 11
Art of the Confederacy: 37–39
Battles
    Antietam (Maryland): 30
    First Manassas (Virginia): 37
Beauregard, Pierre G.T.: 29
Bell, John: 18
Benjamin, Judah: 28, 29
Black Hawk (Sauk chief): 8
Bowser, Mary Elizabeth: 35–36
Bragg, Braxton: 29
Breckinridge, John C.: 18
Calhoun, John C.: 21, 23
Confederate States of America: 13, 22, 23, 26–30,
    31–34, 37–39
Cotton: 6, 19, 20, 29, 31, 32, 33
Davis, Jefferson
    childhood: 4–6
    children: 13–14, 16, 43
    education: 4–6, 7–9
    homes: 4–6, 12–13, 15–16, 26, 35–36, 41–42
    military career: 7–9, 10–11, 16
    political career: 13, 15–18
    post–Civil War: 40–42
    president, Confederate States of America:
        13, 22, 26–30, 32, 37, 39
    siblings: 4, 6, 12
Davis, Samuel: 4–6
Davis, Sarah Knox Taylor: 9, 12
Davis, Varina Anne ("Winnie"): 13,14, 43
Davis, Varina Banks Howell: 12–14, 16, 26, 28, 40, 41
Declaration of Independence: 15
Douglas, Stephen A.: 17, 18
Emancipation Proclamation: 30
Florida (Confederate ship): 33
Fort Monroe (Virginia): 13, 40
Grant, Ulysses S.: 30
Greeley, Horace: 41
Hinds family: 5
Howell, Joseph Davis: 9
Jackson, Andrew: 5, 6, 23

Jackson, Thomas "Stonewall": 38, 39
Jamestown (Virginia): 19
Jefferson, Thomas: 4
Johnson, Andrew: 13
Johnston, Albert: 29
Johnston, Joseph E.: 29
Kearsarge (Union ship): 31, 34
Lee, Robert E.: 29, 30, 40
Lincoln, Abraham: 18, 22, 30
Mallory, Stephen: 28
McNiven, Thomas: 35–36
Memminger, Christopher: 28
Missouri Compromise: 20, 22
Native Americans: 8, 16, 17
Naval engagements: 31–34
Nullification: 21, 23
Pemberton, J.C.: 29
Pierce, Franklin: 16, 17
Reagan, John H.: 28
Richmond (Virginia): 13, 30, 35–36, 38–39,
    40, 42, 43
Robert E. Lee (Confederate ship): 33
Secession: 18, 22, 23, 28
Seddon, James A.: 30
Shenandoah (Confederate ship): 34
Slavery: 19–20, 22, 23, 27, 30
Spying: 35–36
Stephens, Alexander H.: 27, 28, 29
Tariffs: 20, 21, 23
Taylor, Zachary: 9, 10, 12
Tobacco: 19, 31
Toombs, Robert: 28
U.S. Army: 8, 16, 21, 29
U.S. Constitution: 23, 27
U.S.–Mexican War: 9, 10–11, 15, 16
Van Lew, Elizabeth: 35–36
Walker, Leroy P.: 28
War of 1812: 5–6
Washington, William D.: 38–39
Weapons: 16, 29, 31
West Point military academy: 7, 16

COBBLESTONE®
The CIVIL WAR Series

Few events in our nation's history have been as dramatic as those leading up to and during the Civil War. People held strong views on each side of the Mason-Dixon line, and the clash of North and South had far-reaching consequences for our country that are still being felt today.

Each 48-page book delivers the solidly researched content *COBBLESTONE®* is known for, written in an engaging manner that is sure to retain the attention of young readers. Perfect for report research or pursuing an emerging interest in the Civil War, these resources will complete your collection of materials on this important topic.

Each sturdy, hardcover volume includes:

- Fair and balanced depictions of people and events
- Well-researched text ■ Historical photographs
- Glossary ■ Time line

$17.95 each

NATION AT WAR: SOLDIERS, SAINTS, AND SPIES	COB67900
YOUNG HEROES OF THE NORTH AND SOUTH	COB67901
ABRAHAM LINCOLN: DEFENDER OF THE UNION	COB67902
GETTYSBURG: BOLD BATTLE IN THE NORTH	COB67903
ANTIETAM: DAY OF COURAGE AND SACRIFICE	COB67904
ROBERT E. LEE: DUTY AND HONOR	COB67905
ULYSSES S. GRANT: CONFIDENT LEADER AND HERO	COB67906
STONEWALL JACKSON: SPIRIT OF THE SOUTH	COB67907
JEFFERSON DAVIS AND THE CONFEDERACY	COB67908
REBUILDING A NATION: PICKING UP THE PIECES	COB67909

Buy 3 books and get our Time Line Poster FREE!

Our books are available through all major wholesalers, as well as directly from us.